W9-AAD-267

10-Day Green Smoothie Cleanse System: Over 80+ All-New Green Smoothie Recipes to lose 15 Lbs. in 10 Days

by Jessy Smith

Copyright © 2014 by: Andry Brown

All rights reserved. This book or any portion thereof may not be reproduced or used in any manner whatsoever without the express written permission of the publisher except for the use of brief quotations in a book review.

Disclaimer:
The information provided in this book is designed to provide helpful information on the subjects discussed. The publisher and author are not responsible for any specific health or allergy needs that may require medical supervision and are not liable for any damages or negative consequences from any treatment, action, application or preparation, to any person reading or following the information in this book.

Table of Contents

Watermelon Mint Smoothie
Salad Classic Green
Avocado Smooth
Classic Lime & Dill Detox
Ultimate Green Tea
Vanilla Tangy Smoothie
Mint Pudding Smoothie
Maximum Cleanse Smoothie
Minted Pear Smoothie
Peachy Dream Smoothie
Avocado Dilly Dally
Pineapple Blueberry Smoothie
Creamy Cabbage Smoothie
Morning Meal Smoothies
Kiwi and Vanilla
Herbal berries Serenade
Skinny & Sexxy Smoothies
Apple wonders
Flow with the Beet
Dill Kiwi Smoothie
Detox super greens
Blueberry Light
Banana Island Smoothies
Strawberry Sunset
Minted Cacao Crème
Gracious Grapes Smoothies
Herbal Ginger Carrot
Kale-berry Green Smoothies
Magic Mint Smoothie

Introduction

I want to specially thank you for taking your time to Buy and read this book and for taking that bold step to change your lifestyle for the Best. You are about to discover an undisclosed secret of losing 15 lbs. in just 10 days using green smoothies in this Easy 10-day green smoothie cleanse guide. Whether you are trying to improve your health, lose weight, get more energy, or clear your skin—one habit that will help you tremendously to achieve your goals quickly and easily is **drinking green smoothies every day**.

Most people know that to be healthy and achieve the ideal weight they should be eating a healthy diet that includes loads of fresh raw fruits and vegetables. However few people are able to actually do that consistently each and every day, so you may need to use some tricks to make it easier for yourself.

That's one of the reasons why green smoothies have been growing in popularity so quickly - they are SUPER HEALTHY, SUPER EASY to make, and SUPER TASTY too!

Getting Started With This 10 Day Green Smoothie Cleanse

Begin with these easy steps to ensure a simple transition (and to experience great benefits from your 10days!).This detox is for both beginners and those already doing this cleanse! We will start by adding green smoothies to your diet. For better results you may want to increase your intake of daily fiber to improve your detox results. It is very simple to add more fiber to your diet, simply add more baked or steamed vegetables to your meals. You can even add raw salads such as cabbage, carrots and beets or you can opt for baked sweet potatoes, parsnips or turnips.

This will be the first step in preparing your body for its daily green smoothie. Share this exciting news with family members and friends. Fill them in on your plans for starting a new daily green smoothie diet. Ask them to fully support you on your decision and to keep you motivated, who knows? Maybe they will join you!

You will have to plan out your 10 day challenge. Schedule some time in between for exercise, like gentle walks, relaxing time like a gentle massage or a long warm bath with aroma candles. These simple and easy steps allow us to do less and therefore we will be more productive. Just for this 10days it will be advisable to rid yourself from all junk food. This detox is not complex- we simply adding green smoothie to your daily diet plan.

7 Ninja Ways to Prevent Food Cravings

1. Take a trip to your local grocery store or local farmers market and purchase all your fruits, greens and vegetables (enough to last you 5 days).The amount you purchase will obviously depend on your individual needs. I personally recommend that you purchase enough stock, especially bananas and greens (unless you are limiting your intake on sweet fruits because of health issues).You will need fruit to give you a great tasting smoothie and to give your body the necessary calories it needs.

2. You will also need some sunflower seeds and walnuts, whole grains, oats, beans and quinoa all can be purchased at your local grocery store. This is a perfect choice for snack time as well as making great tasting vegetable meals and of course meal replacement smoothies. There are many fruits and veggies that do not provide you with the much needed calories to get through your day, and now is not the time to be starving, as this will only lead to disaster.

3. This is how you are going to succeed: Whenever the thought crosses your mind for having a bowl of delicious ice cream or a yummy donut, you will opt for a delicious smoothie instead! You can even make your

smoothie from frozen fruits, it makes a perfect dessert! Best way to go about this is to visualize it; you can see it right in front of you and taste the sweet delicious fruits inside your mouth. Picture this in your mind and at the same time you feel the excess fat leaving your body. What a great feeling!

4. When the hunger strikes and you are craving all your favorite goodies like your chocolates and chip and dips, beat it with a karate chop by taking a delicious mouthwatering sweet green smoothie. Your body will be very thankful and this feeling that you can accomplish this will soon become a routine.

5. For those times when you are craving a cooked meal, be ready and have some vegetable soup at hand, you can have a salad for your side dish or even some steamed or cooked veggies or whole grains. Beans with rice are also great choice or even easy whole grain pasta with your steamed veggies and a delicious tomato sauce.

6. When you're cravings arise, do not avoid them, and just let yourself know that you will have them at a later stage, AFTER you have had your delicious green smoothie. You are allowed to have a small portion of the food that you are craving. Pay close attention to these foods, the

textures, colors, taste and appearance. Have you noticed the way these foods makes you feel? I do not want you to be left with a guilty feeling, just stay alert and remember how these foods will affect your body.

7.   Acknowledge the new person that you always wanted to be: glowing, slim, full of energy, confident and excited about life.

Tips for a Successful 10 Day cleanse

1. Stock up on your ingredients. You will need lots of fruits, veggies and greens for at least 4-5 days. This way you will not be tempted to eat other things.

2. You can drink as many green smoothies as you desire.

3. You can prepare your days green smoothies in advance preferably in the mornings; this will be a time saver!

4. Your daily 8 glasses of water is still essential. You can drink them in between.

5. In addition to your green smoothies, you are allowed to have:

    - Any raw or green salads.
    - Fresh pressed veggie juice.
    - Raw vegetables.
    - Raw fruits.

- Raw nuts (not roasted/salted) - small amounts (only 1/4 cup per day).

- This detox can continue for an additional 3-5 days, or even longer, it's your choice! After this I suggest that you return to consuming clean meals containing proteins in stage 2.

If you experience any negative effects (like a cleansing reaction), reduce your green smoothie intake for a while, drink plenty of water and give your body a good rest. In the next section you will find some tips on what to do if you should experience a cleansing reaction.

How to Deal with the cleanse Side Effect

How to Cope with Negative Effects Natural Cleanse Reactions on Green Smoothie Diet?

If it has been a while since you have been on a high plant diet, and you have been indulging in caffeine, processed foods, unhealthy fats etc., you might be among those few people that are experiencing some unpleasant cleansing reactions when they begin to take their green smoothie. Among those reactions you can expect the following:

- Digestive disturbances.

- Headaches.

- Skin rashes or breakouts.

- Feeling of weakness.

- Mood swings.

- Mucus in the back of the throat.

- Intestinal gas.

- And other

I know what you are thinking right now: Your very reason for taking green smoothies was so that you can see some good results; instead you end up feeling miserable. I too was in this same position. When I first made the decision to begin a plant based diet, quitting sugar, coffee, all white flour products and many other things that was not good for my body all at the same time, of course back then I had no idea about green smoothie. I went through a phase where I had terrible headaches, terrible body aches and I was feeling very tired each day for about a week.

I spend most of my time during these days in bed and I drank plenty of water. It was only up until last year that I stumbled upon the incredible green smoothie, but yet again I had to undergo another cleansing, only this time I had plenty of mucus coming out my body and it lasted for about three weeks.

For both these cleansing phases it didn't take much time to pass, but I can just imagine how difficult it must be to function while something like this is happening to you. Do not despair as most of these side effects do not last very long. Sometimes it only takes a few weeks or even days, especially if you follow all these below tips accordingly for a healthy cleanse in the section that follows.

What Can I Do About a Cleansing Reaction?

If you have a really bad feeling in terms of functioning properly, it's best to reduce your green smoothie intake for a few days. You should be able to acknowledge these symptoms of discomfort as it can be a good thing, but be sure not to avoid your great new daily routine.

Drink plenty of water; this will help in eliminating all toxins that is unwanted. The average 8 glasses of water will do the trick! If possible stay relaxed for a couple of days get some sleep and enough rest. You will eventually start to regain your energy sooner than you think.

Note: *if you have really terrible reactions or they bother you in some way, it will be advisable to consult your health practitioner to ensure that you are cleansing in a safe method, especially if you may have some health concerns.*

12 Best tips For a Healthy Cleanse

1. Only make use of organic fruits and greens for your smoothie. There are over billion pounds of pesticides that are released into the environment each year in the USA alone.

2. Add plenty of raw veggies and fruits to your green smoothie, your salads, soups and juices.

3. Drink at least 8 glasses of water a day, this will ensure that you get rid of those extra toxins faster. You should also drink infusions using ginger, lemon, star anise, fennel, milk thistle and certain herbs made with hot or warm water.

4. Avoid processed foods, caffeine, smoking, complex sugars and alcohol. If you happen to have an addiction to alcohol, cigarettes and caffeine, these issues should be addressed on its own.

5. Avoid all animal foods- dairy, seafood and meat completely during your cleansing period and even after that.

6. Adding fresh lemon juice and ginger to your smoothie is a great idea!

7. Avoid all chemical based household products as well as all health care products like shampoos, toothpaste and deodorants; opt for a more natural alternative instead.

8. Get enough rest and limit stressful conditions along with detoxifying your body. Meditation and yoga are both very effective methods to help in relieving stress.

9. Make use of a sauna, this way your body can sweat out and get rid of all waste.

10. You can dry-brush your skin to remove toxins through your pores.

11. Exercise is always a good option. Jumping works best. Either take a skipping rope or jump on a trampoline; this will help in cleansing your lymphatic system.

12. Massage your colon. In the mornings, use either your hands or a ball to deeply massage your colon. You can begin with your lower right in your pelvis, then go straight up to the level of your navel, move straight across a couple of inches inside the left hipbone and then down again.

.

Bear in mind that this situation is just a temporary one and that your body is doing excellent, necessary work and best of all you are **BURNING FAT**, getting rid of toxins, and the discomfort is only for a while. If your goal is to lose weight, you will soon see results. When you replace your high-calorie foods with low calorie, high nutrition foods like your green smoothies, you will soon be losing weight. You will feel more energetic and excited about life to.

Green Smoothies for Kids & The Entire Family

Are your kids fussy when it comes to eating their veggies?

Would they have candy instead over a piece of fresh fruit?

Are they among those who are lacking all proteins and nutrients needed for their growing bodies?

If this is the case, you are not alone! There are MANY parents, like you, that are struggling with the exact same problem.

These parents are especially concerned about the lack of veggies and fruits that their kids are eating and with good reason...the modern convenience food markets are lacking all nutritional value that the kids so desperately need. This is why so many kids are not developing the taste or cravings for those nutritional foods that their little bodies need most...fresh leafy veggies and fruits.

All parents want their kids to be healthy without falling prey to the SAD (Standard American Diet), but if you are struggling to get them to eat their fruits and vegetables what can you do?

Kids Are Crazy About Green Smoothies!

One of the greatest things about green smoothies is that they tend to hide all those little ingredients that seem to be unfavorable to our little ones. Many kids are crazy about these smoothies from the moment they take a sip, and there is no need for them to know that they are drinking their fruits and vegetables unless you let the secret get out! If it is spinach or kale that your kids are struggling to eat at dinner time, you will be amazed how well they drink it in a smoothie.

You can give your little ones a green smoothie in the mornings or you can serve it in between meals every day, this way you will have the peace of mind, knowing that your kids are filled with the nutrition that they deserve.

Green smoothies is best for your kids as it ensures that they receive the needed nutrition- greens, fruits, protein, fiber, calcium and all other nutrients that the little bodies need to grow big and strong. Green smoothies also have a delicious taste to it. Kids can be picky eaters and you will love the fact that these recipes can disguise those very important dark leafy greens.

How to get your kids to fall in love with green smoothies?

From my personal experience, the majority of kids love the green smoothie right from the start. The more fussy ones will need some convincing. Below you will find a motivational method to get your kids (and you) more excited about eating lots of greens. You will find that this method can be used for a number of different things, for instance, it works very well with exercise. This is an adaption of the "Foot in the Door Strategy." If your kid is refusing to drink the green smoothie, begin by first making a smoothie that doesn't appear green at all.

You can begin with a smoothie that contains lots of natural sweeteners and plenty of fruit. Kids are crazy about the sweet delicious taste of ripe fruit. Once you got this part covered, sparingly start to incorporate celery into your green smoothie. Celery doesn't have any effect on the color or taste of your green smoothie and this is a perfect way to get your kids to start eating more nutritional veggies. Your kids may be curious about what are inside the green smoothie, but do not let them know. Even if your kids do not love it, they sure will not hate it either. When your kids are used to the celery, you can add small amounts of other greens to the smoothie. By adding other color ingredients, like blueberries, it will help disguise the color that a few kids may see as a problem.

After a while, the entire family will get used to the delicious taste of the smoothie and will even prefer it over the no vegetable version. Your taste buds can be very adaptable! So take note: the best green to begin with is celery, as it doesn't allow your smoothie to appear too green, and it gives a mild flavor when combined with fruit.

Tips To Get Your Kids Going With Green Smoothies

Here are some additional tips to help you get your kids going with green smoothies:

1. Make it a fun routine. Let your kids name their smoothies. Magic Potion, Green Power Ninja and Princess Nectar all make great fun smoothie names! You can let your imagination run wild with this one.

2. Get your kids involve by letting them help you prepare the smoothies. With your supervision allow them to use the blender and add fruits and veggies to their smoothie.

3. Take the kids along when shopping for the ingredients for the smoothie. Give them the chance to pick the veggies and fruits.

4. Freeze your smoothie into a Popsicle container.

5. Pour the smoothie into a pretty glass add an umbrella and straw. A colored glass will be even better to hide the color of the smoothie.

6. Let your kid have a green smoothie first thing in the mornings, before anything else and stick to this routine. Another smoothie should be given 1 and half hours prior to dinner time. A fresh fruit can also be given as a special treat.

7. Teach your little ones about the importance of eating vegetables and fruit. Use simple words so that they can easily understand. You will be amazed at how eager they are to learn.

8. Praise your kids whenever they drink a green smoothie.

9. Become a role model. If you are always on a diet of have bad eating habits, your kids will grow up to think that this is a normal and healthy way of living.

10. If all else fail, rewards works best! I'm personally no fan of the reward system, but we must do what works best. Avoid using junk food as a reward by all means.

Green Smoothies FAQs

How can you fix a smoothie that you are not crazy about?

This hardly happens, but it does. So you made a smoothie and you don't really love it. Do not feel hopeless. The benefits of smoothies over any other kind of recipes, is that smoothies can be easily fixed.

Simply add more liquid.

"My smoothie end up too watery":

Add more vegetables and fruits. Avocados and bananas work best when you want to make a delicious thick and creamy smoothie.

"My smoothie end up too savory":

Add additional sweet fruits. Add sweetener or a packet of stevia, 1-2 tablespoons agave syrup. Adding a few pieces of dried fruit can also work, but then you must make sure that you mix it really well.

"My smoothie end up too sweet":

Add some fresh lemon or lime juice to the smoothie. Add additional celery or greens and blend together.

"My smoothie tastes too bland":

It could be that the ingredients you have added do not complement one another, or that there is not enough ingredients with distinct taste. For whatever reason adding cinnamon, spices, fresh ginger, fresh lemon, mint leaves and vanilla always seems to help. This will add an instant flavor to a bland smoothie.

"My smoothie end up too "green" tasting":

Plenty of greens have a very distinct flavor. If you added mustard greens or dandelion, which are both strong tasting greens, you are going to have to dilute your smoothie by adding additional fruits, ginger or lemon and mild greens.

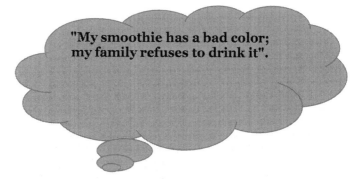

"My smoothie has a bad color; my family refuses to drink it".

Best way to disguise the color of your smoothie is by adding coco powder or a few frozen blueberries. Another way will be to serve it in a colored glass with a straw.

Peel or Not?

If you are an owner of a high-speed blender, there is no need to organic fruits like kiwis, mangoes, pears and apples. You can blend pears and apples with its seeds inside. If you just have an ordinary blender that runs on a slow speed, seeds and peels will not completely blend and this might destroy your blender, however with a high- speed blender you can blend just about anything. It is best to peel fruit that are not grown organically.

Storing Green Smoothies

"Can you store green smoothies? How long do they last in the refrigerator? "Your green smoothie can be stored either in your refrigerator or freezer. It can last up to 3 days in the refrigerator and 3 months in your freezer.

Please remember that you should take out your frozen smoothie several hours before using it, always shake well before drinking. It's best to drink your smoothie soon after you have had your meal to get better taste and nutrition.

How Many Smoothies Must I Drink Per Day?

There is no limit to the amount of smoothies you can drink per day, so you are allowed to enjoy as many as you wish. There are times when I only drink one quarter, than other days I find myself drinking two, three and at times even four in a single day!

Maximum & Modified Cleanse

The maximum cleanse consist of three green smoothies a day, here the green smoothies are used for meal replacement and can help you lose the "maximum weight" of about 10 to 15 lbs. This is for those looking to lose weight fast, and would follow through consistently for the 10 days. You would have to commit 10 days of not eating refined sugars, sodas, processed foods, fried foods and refined carbs then the weight will happen naturally giving you more energy and motivation to lose weight effortlessly.

On the other hand, in Modified cleanse, you would have to take green smoothies two times a day, for breakfast and lunch, while you take clean healthy protein meals for dinner. Here the weight does not come off fast, but gradually. This is for those looking to try these cleanse, without following through the 10 days cleanse.

Nevertheless, for this to work effectively, you would stop eating any meal that contains refined sugars, sodas, processed foods, fried foods and refined carbs then the weight will come off naturally and you would begin to experience magical changes in your health. Remember, this cleanse is not a diet But a lifestyle.

Below are some delicious and healthy green smoothies that would help you achieve your weight loss goal in no time!

Please note; Most of these recipes makes for 2 servings.

Now, unto the recipes, Enjoy:

Maximum Cleanse Recipes

Watermelon Mint Smoothie

The ultimate hydrator, this refreshing Watermelon mint smoothie is perfect for refueling after a workout or for taking to the beach on a hot and humid day. (The lycopene in the watermelon will actually help protect your skin from sunburn!)

Ingredients:

2 cups cubed seedless watermelon
1 whole cucumber, peeled, seeded, and coarsely chopped
1 large handful chopped kale
3 tablespoons fresh lime juice
1/4 cup chopped fresh mint
1/4 cup chopped fresh basil
1 cup ice cubes

How you make it:

1. Place the watermelon and cucumber in a blender, and blend until creamy and smooth.
2. Add the remaining ingredients and process again.
3. Drink ice cold.

Salad Classic Green

This one's packed with many great ingredients, almost like a liquid salad. The sweetness is mild and comes from the beet and carrot. The basic smoothie is really quite mild. Because it's more green and less sweet it seems to be better for green smoothie aficionados. The parsley, ginger and lime lift it. For more taste bud action add in some cayenne and cumin.

Ingredients:

1 cup water
¼ cup beet chopped
¼ cup carrot chopped small
Small amount ginger
½ avocado
1 cup mild greens (spinach, kale, choy, sweet potato leaves)
1 cup strong greens (rocket, watercress or mustard leaves)
¼ cup cilantro/coriander
1 cup parsley
Sea salt
2 tbsp. lime juice
1 cup ice and blend again

How you make it:

1. First, Place beet, carrot, water and small amount of ginger into blender and blend until mixture is a green juice-like consistency.
2. Stop blender and add avocado, greens with the other remaining ingredients and blend.
3. Add 1 cup of ice and blend again until creamy.

Tips

To green it up even more add a stalk of celery or a cup of broccoli
Add some cayenne pepper and cumin

Avocado Smooth

The smoothness of avocado balanced with sweet, salty and tangy flavors with a touch of cilantro.

Ingredients:

1 cup water
½ cup pineapple
½ large avocado
2 tomatoes
½ cup red bell pepper
1 1/2 cups greens
½ cup cucumber
¼ cup coriander
1 tbsp. lime juice
Pinch cayenne pepper (to taste)
Pinch sea salt
Ice

How you make it:

1. Place all the ingredients into blender and blend until mixture is a green juice-like consistency.
2. Add ice and blend again until creamy.

Tips.

To make the smoothie smoother, mild and strong add 1.5 cup of greens
Add more lime juice to increase the tang!

Classic Lime & Dill Detox

Here, dill adds a sweet, fresh flavor while also contributing an abundance of antioxidants to this creamy Super Green smoothie.

Ingredients:

1/2 pear
1 cup chopped and seeded cucumber
1/4 cup chopped fresh dill
1 small avocado
1 cup baby spinach
2 tablespoons lime juice
1-inch knob fresh gingerroot, peeled
1 cup frozen pineapplc
11/4 cups water
3 to 4 ice cubes

How you make it:

1. Place all the ingredients except the ice in a blender, and blend until smooth and creamy.
2. Add the ice and process again. Drink chilled.

Ultimate Green Tea

Now you can get your green tea and greens all in one! This Drink would keep your skin glowing every day.

Ingredients:

1 Anjou pear, chopped
1/4 cup white raisins (or dried mulberries)
1 teaspoon freshly minced gingerroot
1 large handful chopped romaine lettuce
1 tablespoon hemp seeds
1 cup unsweetened brewed green tea, cooled
7 to 9 ice cubes

How you make it:

1. Place all the ingredients except the ice in a Blender, and process until smooth and creamy.
2. Add ice if desired and process again.
3. Serve and Drink chilled.

Vanilla Tangy Smoothie

This smoothie (which unbelievably the best ever tasted) is packed with nutritious brazil nuts, avocado and of course a mountain of leafy greens. It will be THICK so to make it drinkable, add more water ½ cup at a time. Actually I like to eat this one with a spoon, like a pudding dessert.
First blend the nuts and water. Then add in the other ingredients.

Ingredients:

½ cup brazil nuts
1 cup water
2 dates (remove the pits of course)
½ avocado
1.5 – 2 tsp vanilla
¼ tsp sea salt
2 cups mild greens (use spinach or chickweed)
Ice if you need it

How you make it:

1. Place all the ingredients into blender and blend until mixture is a green juice-like consistency.
2. Add ice and blend again until creamy.

Tips

Instead of dates add dried peaches or apricots for even more nutrition. Soak them (adding soak water too) if you want them very smooth.

Mint Pudding Smoothie

If you want to drink this delicious smoothie, keep adding water until you get your desired consistency. It's beautifully suited to using a spoon and savoring every last mouthful.

Ingredients:

½ cup brazil nuts
1 cup water
2 dates
½ avocado
1.5 – 2 tsp vanilla
¼ tsp salt
1 cup mild greens (use spinach or chickweed)
1 cup mint
Ice, if you will!

How you make it:

1. Place all the ingredients into blender and blend until mixture is a green juice-like consistency.
2. Add ice and blend again until creamy.

Tips

Instead of dates add dried peaches or apricots for even more nutrition. Soak them (adding soak water too) if you want them very smooth.

Maximum Cleanse Smoothie

This smoothie is great in its own way. It helps detox your body, with the flavor of collard greens and celery stalks, you can't go wrong with this drink.

Ingredients:

2 cups collard greens
2 celery stalks
1 cucumber
2 pears
1/2 inch ginger
1 lemon
1 cup water

How you make it:

1. Place the collard and water into blender and blend until mixture is a green juice-like consistency.
2. Stop blender and add the other remaining ingredients and blend.
3. Add ice if desired and blend again until creamy.

Minted Pear Smoothie

As usual there are 2 cups of salad leaves in this recipe! The strength of the cress or other strong leaves really lends this smoothie a pleasing bite. Feel free to change the proportions of the strong leaves to taste.

Ingredients:

1 cup water
½ cup broccoli
1 pear
¼ - ½ cup mint
1 cup mild leaves such as baby spinach
1 cup strong leaves such as watercress
Ice and water in just the right amounts!

How you make it:

1. Place all the ingredients into blender and blend until mixture is a green juice-like consistency.
2. Add ice and blend again until creamy.

Peachy Dream Smoothie

This creamy dreamy treat is so tasty it can even be eaten as "ice cream"; simply transfer the smoothie into 4 small ramekins and freeze for about 10 minutes.

Ingredients:

1/2 avocado
1 cup frozen organic frozen peaches
1 frozen banana, cut into pieces
2 tablespoons fresh lemon juice
11/4 cups water
Handful of kale
3 to 4 ice cubes
Optional: 2 to 3 pitted dates

How you make it:

1. Place all the ingredients except the ice in a Blender, and blend until smooth and creamy.
2. Add the ice and dates (if using) and process again. Drink chilled.

Avocado Dilly Dally

Ingredients:
1 cup kale
1 cup water
¼ cup dill
1 tomato
1 tbsp. lime juice
1 cup bok or pak choy (don't feel constrained. If you don't have kale and choy, just use 2 cups mild greens.
Remember to vary your green intake)
½ avocado
OPTIONAL: 1 1/2 cups pineapple

How you make it:
1. Place kale, choy and water into blender and blend until mixture is a green juice-like consistency.
2. Stop blender and add remaining ingredients.
3. Blend until creamy.
4. Add ice and water for desired temperature and consistency

Pineapple Blueberry Smoothie

The complement of greens in this smoothie is made up of celery, cilantro and the mild green of your choice.

Ingredients:

1 cup pineapple
2 tomatoes
1 cup blueberries (frozen or fresh)
¼ cup coriander
1 cup spinach leaves or other mild leafy green
1 stick celery chopped
1 squeeze of lemon to taste

How you make it:

1. Place leafy greens and water into blender and blend until mixture is a green juice-like consistency.
2. Stop blender and add remaining ingredients.
3. Blend until creamy.
4. Add ice as required

Creamy Cabbage Smoothie

Ingredients:

1 cup spinach
1 cup cabbage
1 celery
1 cup almond milk
2 packets of stevia
1 cup of ice

How you make it:
1. Place all the ingredients into blender and blend until mixture is a green juice-like consistency.
2. Add the cup of ice and blend again until creamy.

Morning Meal Smoothies

These smoothies can be used for meal Replacement.

Ingredients:
2-4 cups baby spinach or kale
1/2 cup any type cooked whole grain or white bean
1 ripe banana
1 tsp. cinnamon
1 tbsp. walnuts
1 1/2 cups water or 1 cup of ice.

How you make it:
1. Place all the ingredients into blender and blend until mixture is a green juice-like consistency.
2. Add the cup of ice and blend again until creamy.

Kiwi and Vanilla

What can I say? This cornucopia of interesting ingredients turns out a delicious high scoring smoothie!

Ingredients:

Handful of almonds
1 cup water
2 dates
1 tsp vanilla essence
2 kiwi
¼ tsp salt
1 cup kale (or mild greens)
½ cup broccoli
Handful of sprouts

How you make it:

1. First, Place the almonds and water into blender and blend until mixture is a green juice-like consistency.
2. Stop blender and add dates, vanilla essence, greens with the other remaining ingredients and blend.
3. Add ice if desired and blend again until creamy.

Tips

If you don't have sprouts on hand just add an extra ½ cup of mild greens. Substitute your dates with dried peaches or apricots for even more nutrition. Soak them (adding soak water too) if you want them very smooth.

Herbal berries Serenade

Adding Herbs to your smoothies is another way to increase your benefits and your green quota. The apple provides just the right amount of sweetness to balance the raspberries and cilantro.

Ingredients:

1 cup water
1 cup raspberries (frozen)
1 apple (minus the stalk, chopped)
¼ cup cilantro/coriander
1 celery stalk
1 1/2 cup mild greens
1 cup of Ice

How you make it:
1. Place all the ingredients into blender and blend until mixture is a green juice-like consistency.
2. Add ice and blend again until creamy.

Tips

For the Mild green, go on, test this out with a small amount of strong greens too and feel the smooth, thick and delicious taste.

Skinny & Sexxy Smoothies

Ingredients:
4 cups spinach
2 apples
1/2 whole lime with peel
2 bananas
1 1/2 cup of water.

How you make it:

1. Place the Spinach and water into the blender and blend until the mixture is a juice-like consistency.
2. Stop the blender and add the remaining ingredients. Blend until creamy.

Apple wonders

Apple is a great fruit that taste really well when used in making smoothie. It has wonderful flavors, which makes drinking green smoothies an ultimate delight.

Ingredients:

4 cups of kale
4 apples
½ lemon juice
1 cup ice

How you make it:
1. First, Place the kale and water into blender and blend until mixture is a green juice-like consistency.
2. Stop blender and add the other remaining ingredients and blend.
3. Add ice if desired and blend again until creamy.

Flow with the Beet

Orange provides some of the liquid so you can only add ½ cup water to start.

Ingredients:

1 orange
¼ cup beet
¼ - ½ cup parsley
1 cups asparagus, spinach or chickweed
1 cup strong (watercress or rocket)
Ginger
1 cup ice

How you make it:

1. Place all the ingredients into blender and blend until mixture is a green juice-like consistency.
2. Add ice and blend again until creamy.

Tips

According to preference. I use 1 cup mild (spinach, asparagus lettuce or chickweed) and 1 cup of strong watercress or rocket to give it a smooth flow of deliciousness.

Dill Kiwi Smoothie

Blend this simply tasty high-scoring smoothie and marvel how dill and kiwi are such great partners.
If your blender is not powerful enough then you may want to chop the little hard bit off the stalk end of your kiwi. I never peel my kiwi for a smoothie because it adds fiber.

Ingredients:

1 cup water
2 cups of mild greens (try bok choy, mizuna or chickweed)
1 stalk celery
¼ cup dill
2 kiwi
1 cup of Ice

How you make it:

1. Place all the ingredients into blender and blend until mixture is a green juice-like consistency.
2. Add ice and blend again until creamy.

Detox super greens

Ingredients:

1/2 head of lettuce
1 cup dandelion greens
2 celery sticks
2 apples
1 banana
1 cup of ice

How you make it:

1. First, Place the lettuce head and water into blender and blend until mixture is a green juice-like consistency.
2. Stop blender and add the other remaining ingredients and blend.
3. Add ice if desired and blend again until creamy.

Blueberry Light

Always refreshing and light. Good for sipping in the summer or while chilling in the beach.

Ingredients:

1 cup water
1 cup blueberries (frozen)
1 apple (without the stalk, chopped)
¼ cup dill
1 celery stalk
1 1/2 cups mild greens
Ice

How you make it:

1. Place all the ingredients into blender and blend until mixture is a green juice-like consistency.
2. Add ice and blend again until creamy.

Banana Island Smoothies

Ingredients:

2-4 cups leaves of green leaf lettuce
2 ripe mangoes, peeled and pit removed
2 apples
1 banana
2 cups of water

How you make it:

1. First, Place the lettuce leaf and water into blender and blend until mixture is a green juice-like consistency.
2. Stop blender and add the other remaining ingredients and blend.
3. Add ice if desired and blend again until creamy.

Strawberry Sunset

This variation on a strawberries is completely different with the addition of a kiwi dill theme.

Ingredients:

1 cup water
1 cup strawberries (frozen or fresh)
2 kiwi
2 cups of mild greens (try bok choy, spinach or chickweed)
1 stalk celery
¼ cup dill
Ice

How you make it:

1. Place all the ingredients into blender and blend until mixture is a green juice-like consistency.
2. Add ice and blend again until creamy.

Minted Cacao Crème

Cacao can be substituted by cacao nibs or carob if you like. It's all good!

Ingredients:

1 cup water
½ cup cashews (soaked if you have them available, dry will do)
3 soft dates (or soaked dried fruit)
Then add:
Up to 2 tbsp. cacao
1 cup mint
1 small avocado, or half a large
1 cup mild greens
¼ - ½ tsp cinnamon optional
Vanilla
Pinch sea salt
1 cup ice

How you make it:

1. First, Place cashew, dates and water into blender and blend until mixture is a green juice-like consistency.
2. Stop blender and add cacao, avocadoes, greens with the other remaining ingredients and blend.
3. Add ice if desired and blend again until creamy.

Gracious Grapes Smoothies

Ingredients:

1/2 head romaine lettuce
2 stalks of celery
1 orange
1 bunch red grapes
1 cup water

How you make it:

1. First, Place the romaine lettuce and water into blender and blend until mixture is a green juice-like consistency.
2. Stop blender and add celery, orange, the red grapes and blend.
3. Add ice if desired and blend again until creamy.

Herbal Ginger Carrot

Ingredients:

I cup water
¼ cup beet chopped
¼ cup carrot chopped small
Small amount ginger
1 cup mild greens (for eg: spinach, kale, choy, sweet potato leaves)
1 cup strong greens (rocket, watercress or mustard leaves)
¼ cup cilantro/coriander
½ cup broccoli
1 cup water
1 cup ice and blend again

How you make it:

1. Place beet, carrot and water into blender and blend until mixture is a green juice-like consistency.
2. Stop blender and add greens with water and blend.
3. Add 1 cup of ice and blend again until creamy.

Tips
If you prefer mild greens? Then use 2 cups. To add taste bud drama, add cayenne and lime juice. Vary the amount of strong greens to your taste.

Kale-berry Green Smoothies

Ingredients:

1 small bunch green kale
1 pint strawberries
3 small peaches
2 cups water

How you make it:

1. Place the green kale and water into blender and blend until mixture is a green juice-like consistency.
2. Stop blender and add the other remaining ingredients and blend.
3. Add ice if desired and blend again until creamy.

Magic Mint Smoothie

This mild-flavored smoothie is great with generous helpings of vanilla, spice and mint. Feel free to add extra mint.

The chia gel (if it's been pre-soaked in water) ups the ante on the protein amount. You'll get way more into your system if you blend the chia with the smoothie. Unblended chia gel really gives a great 'bubble tea' texture that's interesting. Actually it's quite alluring for children!

Ingredients:

1 cup water
½ large avocado
4 dates
Vanilla 1 tsp essence or ½ tsp powder (or more to taste)
½ tsp cinnamon
½ tsp nutmeg
1.5 cups greens of your choice (mild greens)
½ cup mint leaves
2 tbsp. chia gel
Ice

How you make it:

1. Place all the ingredients into blender and blend until mixture is a green juice-like consistency.
2. Add ice and blend again until creamy.

Tips

You can add a pinch of clove or cardamom powder if you are partial to nutmegs. Also, for the chia gel, either blend or stir in after for the texture of a bubble tea.

Dried peaches or apricots or raisins can be used instead of dates. They are more nutritious. Soak them (adding soak water too) if you want them very smooth.

Brussels Blaster Smoothie

Lovely Smoothie you can Enjoy with the whole family and they'll love it

Ingredients:
12 Brussels sprouts
1 yellow grapefruit, peeled
2 cups mixed berries, frozen
2 bananas, frozen
1 apple
1 cup any type cooked whole grain or white bean
Stevia or agave to taste (optional)
3 cups water/ice

How you make it:
1. First, Place the Brussel sprout and ice into blender and blend until mixture is a green juice-like consistency.
2. Stop blender and add celery, orange, the red grapes and blend.
3. Add ice if desired and blend again until creamy.

Green Accolades

This is the clean and healthy of a piña colada! It detox the body and help you lose weight easily. Who don't like a delicious and healthy smoothie?

Ingredients:

1 cup frozen chopped pineapple
3 tablespoons raw, unsweetened, shredded coconut
1 tablespoon fresh lime juice
1 handful baby spinach leaves
3 pitted dates
1 cup water
4 to 5 ice cubes

How you make it:

1.   Place all the ingredients except the ice in a blender, and blend thoroughly until smooth and creamy.
2.   Add the ice and process again.
3.   Drink ice cold.

Avocado Ascent

Ingredients:

1 avocado
1 large cucumber
2 cups spinach
4 large green leaves (collards, kale, etc)
2-3 lemons, juice only (to taste)
1 1/2 cups water

How you make it:

1. Place all the ingredients into blender and blend until mixture is a green juice-like consistency.
2. Add the cup of ice and blend again until creamy & smooth.

Optional: a dash of stevia or a few slices of apples

Southern Beach Smoothies

Ingredients:

½ bunch Romaine
2 cups strawberries
2 bananas
2 cups water

How you make it:

1.   First, Place the romaine and water into blender and blend until mixture is a green juice-like consistency.
2.   Stop blender and add the other remaining ingredients and blend.
3.   Add ice if desired and blend again until creamy.

Carob Pudding Smoothie

You Got it right... it looks very similar to *Vanilla Pudding,* but that's just on paper. But it is different and it is SO good you need to know how to make this one in its own right.

Ingredients:

1 cup water
½ cup cashews (soaked if you have them available, dry will do)
3 dates (no stone. Or other dried fruit)
2 tbsp. carob
1 small avocado, or ½ large
2 cups mild greens
¼ - ½ tsp cinnamon
Vanilla
Pinch sea salt
1 cup ice or as needed

How you make it:

1. First, Place the cashews, dates and water into blender and blend until mixture is a green juice-like consistency.
2. Stop blender and add carob, green with the other remaining ingredients and blend.
3. Add 1 cup of ice and blend again until creamy.

Tips
Add dried peaches or apricots, instead of dates for even more nutrition. Soak them (adding soak water too) if you want them very smooth.

Lettuce lite Smoothie

A very healthy smoothie that helps keep the bone stronger because of the calcium content in lettuce.

Ingredients:

1 small pineapple, peeled, cored, and chopped
1 large mango, peeled, cored, and chopped
1 small head romaine
lettuce a tiny piece of fresh
ginger
1 cup of ice

How you make it:

1. First, Place the lettuce and water into blender and blend until mixture is a green juice-like consistency.
2. Stop blender and add the other remaining ingredients and blend.
3. Add ice if desired and blend again until creamy.

Parsley Refresher

Lots of green stuff, tons of flavor. Fennel definitely makes this a taste sensation. The salt gives it a flavor boost. Try it.

Ingredients:

1 stalk celery
1 pear
½ cup fennel
1 cup parsley
1 cup greens of your choice
1-2 tbsp. lemon optional
1 cup water
Pinch sea salt
Add ½ cup ice

How you make it:

1. Place all the ingredients into blender and blend until mixture is a green juice-like consistency.
2. Add ice and blend again until creamy.

Sunrise Mint Smoothies

Healthy Smoothie for every waking Day. Keeps you healthy and gives you energy all day long. Your kids would surely love this.

Ingredients:

4 cups of kale
½ bunch of mint
4 ripe pears
2 cups water

How you make it:

1. Mix the kale and water into blender and blend until mixture is a green juice-like consistency.
2. Stop blender and add the other remaining ingredients and blend.
3. Add ice if desired and blend again until creamy.

Modified Cleanse Smoothie

Sunshine Beach smoothie

This Smoothie as it's called is gushing with vitamin C, this energizing drink is the perfect alternative to your morning break!

Ingredients:

1 orange, peeled and chopped
1 kiwi, peeled and chopped
5 pitted dates
1/2 cup frozen pineapple
2 tablespoons hemp seeds
1/2 cup water
3 to 4 ice cubes

How you make it:

1. Place all the ingredients except the ice in a blender, and blend until smooth and creamy.
2. Add the ice and process again.
3. Drink chilled.

Orange Magic Smoothie

The health benefits of oranges are countless. Devour this smoothie with all ravishment. Enjoy the magic in this delicious drink

Ingredients:

1/2 head romaine
2 stalks of celery
1 cup papaya
1 orange
1 cup of red grapes
2 cups water

How you make it:

1. Mix the romaine head and water into blender and blend until mixture is a green juice-like consistency.
2. Stop blender and add other remaining ingredients and blend.
3. Add ice if desired and blend again until creamy.

Ginger Dill Elixir

My family are so much in love with this. What a great lime color! Yeah baby!

Ingredients:

1 pear
½ cucumber (or 1 cup)
¼ cup dill
1 small avocado or half a large
1 cup mild greens (sweet potato or kale)
1 stalk celery
1-3 tbsp. lime juice
Ginger, to taste
Ice

How you make it:

1.   Place all the ingredients into blender and blend until mixture is a green juice-like consistency.
2.   Add ice and blend again until creamy.

Tips

For the lime juice, start with 1 tbsp. and work upwards to taste

Shapelicious Smoothies

Ingredients:

4 leaves kale
2 celery stalks
2 bananas
1 cup of strawberries or blueberries or raspberries
2 cups of water

How you make it:

1. First, Place the kale and water into blender and blend until mixture is a green juice-like consistency.
2. Stop blender and add the other remaining ingredients and blend.
3. Add ice if desired and blend again until creamy.

Orange Energizer

Even though you don't like oranges, you would definitely love this Smoothie drink. Good For the Modified Cleanse.

Ingredients:

1 orange
1 stalk celery
2 cups mild greens
1 cup water
2 dates
Add ½ cup ice

How you make it:

1. Place all the ingredients into blender and blend until mixture is a green juice-like consistency.
2. Add the cup of ice and blend again until creamy.

Tips
For the mild greens, you can try romaine/cos or mizuna or your choice from the list.
Optional – I like to add the dates last in the blend to feel the sweet specks of fruit. If you prefer to avoid dates, the result will be good with other dried fruit. For example add soaked dried peaches or apricots.

Pine-Mint Smoothie

This green smoothie recipe is simple and reliably delicious and good for a newbie to green smoothies. It is indeed a classic. 2 cups is a lot of pineapple so it's best to use a sweet(ish) one. If it's too acid or sour then add more leaves and some sweetener. You could add dried figs or apricots or soft dates.

Ingredients:

1 cup mint leaves
1 cup water
2 cups pineapple (fresh or frozen)
1 cup of spinach leaves or other mild green
1 avocado

How you make it:

1. Place leafy greens and water into blender and blend until mixture is a green juice-like consistency.
2. Stop blender and add remaining ingredients.
3. Blend until creamy.
4. Add ice and extra water to get to your desired temperature and consistency.

Andre's Punch

My beloved kid loved and named this one! You are most definitely right! I bet you guessed that little fact already. You can trust that if Andre wanted to name it that it scored top marks

Ingredients:

1 apple
1 cup pineapple
1 1/2 cup nut milk
¼ cup cilantro/coriander
2 cups mild greens
Ice

How you make it:

1.   Place all the ingredients into blender and blend until mixture is a green juice-like consistency.
2.   Add ice and blend again until creamy.

Tips

For the nut milk, you can use a small handful each of macadamia and walnut added to 1 cup of water

Lime-Oats Delight

Ingredients:

2 cups almond milk
2 bananas, fresh or frozen
2 cups leafy greens (spinach, Swiss chard, kale, etc.)
1 handful of parsley
2 tablespoons sunflower seeds (or other seeds or nuts that you have)
¼ cup of dates (or any other dried fruit)
1 cup oat, brown rice or oat

Juice and zest of 4 limes.

1 cup of ice

How you make it:

1.   Place all the ingredients into blender and blend until mixture is a green juice-like consistency.

2.   Add the cup of ice and blend again until creamy.

Poppy Sunshine Smoothie

This one has all the fruit that my grandma would love if she were with us. It's a kind of memorial smoothie in my house. You'll need ice if all your fruit is fresh and not frozen.

Ingredients:

½ cup mango
½ cup guava (I use frozen guava pulp)
½ cup pineapple
½ cup raspberries
½ cup blueberries
1.5 cups Coconut water
Sea salt
2 pieces of dried fruit (apricot, peach or some raisins, soaked if you like)
2 cups mild greens
½ cup cilantro/coriander
Ice

How you make it:

1. Place all the ingredients into blender and blend until mixture is a green juice-like consistency.
2. Add ice and blend again until creamy.

Delicious Dill Smoothies

Bok choy are green leaves used in making smoothies. They are very nutritious and dark. The darker the smoothie the more nutritious.

Ingredients:

1/2 bunch of Bok Choy
1/2 a bunch of fresh dill
3 bananas
2 celery stalks
2 cups water

How you make it:

1. First, Place the Bok Choy and water into blender and blend until mixture is a green juice-like consistency.
2. Stop blender and add the other remaining ingredients and blend.
3. Add ice if desired and blend again until creamy.

Chilled Carrot Smoothie

Ingredients:

2 oranges, peeled
2 large, organic carrots, chopped
1 apple
½ to 1 inch ginger to taste
1/2 cup chilled water

How you make it:

1. Place all the ingredients into blender and blend until mixture is a green juice-like consistency.
2. Add the cup of ice and blend again until creamy.

Tips

You may want to squeeze the oranges and just use the juice—the consistency will be less thick.

I just use the oranges whole and add some water.

This smoothie is great chilled, so you may want to toss in some ice.

Blend in a high speed blender

Bold Berry Smoothie

The sweetness of bananas, the tang of raspberries and the color of blueberries.

Ingredients:

1 cup water
¼ cup (soaked) almonds
1 cup raspberries
¼ cup blueberries
1 banana
½ cup broccoli
1 small-medium tomato
1 1/2 cup spinach leaves
1 cup of Ice

How you make it:

1. First, Place almonds and water into blender and blend until mixture is a green juice-like consistency.
2. Stop blender and add raspberries, blueberries with the other remaining ingredients and blend.
3. Add ice and blend again until creamy.

Mixed Gazpacho

This smoothie is used as meal replacement and they taste really good and fulfilling.

Ingredients:

2-4 cups greens (kale, collards, parsley, or other)
2-3 stalks of celery
1/4 small avocado
1 cup mixed berries, frozen
1 apple, cored and chopped
1 banana
1 cup cooked beans
2 cups water or non-dairy milk
1 cup of ice

How you make it:

1.   Place all the ingredients into blender and blend until mixture is a green juice-like consistency.
2.   Add the cup of ice and blend again until creamy.

Top Green Smoothie

Make these Delicious Smoothies Today. Blend up a delicious carrot, beet, or radish tops recipe that the whole family will enjoy!

Ingredients:

1 cup radish leaves
2 cups spinach
1 ripe banana, peeled
1 cup mango
1 cup pineapple
1 1/2 cup water or 1 cup of ice

How you make it:

1. Place all the ingredients into blender and blend until mixture is a green juice-like consistency.
2. Add the cup of ice and blend again until creamy.

Chu-Mango Smoothie

Now, Turn On your green light!

Ingredients:

Blend first
1 cup water
8 Brazil nuts (or use a cup of nut milk)
2 cups mild greens (in any combination)
1 cup frozen mango
½ avocado
Vanilla
1 tsp cinnamon, ½ tsp nutmeg
¼ cup cacao nibs (or some cacao powder to taste)
1 cup ice

How you make it:

1.   First, Place Brazil nuts or nut milk and water into blender and blend until mixture is a green juice-like consistency.
2.   Stop blender and add frozen mango, green with the other remaining ingredients and blend.
3.   Add 1 cup of ice and blend again until creamy.

Tips

Add ½ cup more mango or 2 pieces of dried fruit, if you need more sweetness. Clove or cardamom powder are other handy spices that complement cinnamon and nutmeg.

Cappuccino Classic

This coffeehouse-style ice-cold smoothie hits the spot when you need a little zip, pep, and go! With lots of health benefit on the go

Ingredients:

1 banana, cut into bite-sized pieces
1/2 cup water
2 tablespoons hemp seeds
8 almonds
1 teaspoon instant espresso powder
1/2 teaspoon cinnamon
1 teaspoon pure vanilla extract
4 prunes
1 1/2 cups ice

How you make it:

1. Place all the ingredients except the ice in a blender, and blend until smooth and creamy.
2. Add the ice and process again.
3. Serve & Drink ice cold.

Salad Sunrise Smoothie

In one blend, you get sweet and savory. The pineapple really does a good job to complement the vegetables here.

Ingredients:

1 cup water
¼ cup beet chopped
¼ cup carrot chopped small
Small amount ginger
1 cup pineapple
½ avocado
2 cups greens (incorporating mild and up to 1 cup strong greens)
¼ cup cilantro/coriander
¼ cup broccoli
1 cup of ice

How you make it:

1. First, Place beet, carrot, water and small amount of ginger into blender and blend until mixture is a green juice-like consistency.
2. Stop blender and add pineapple, greens with the other remaining ingredients and blend.
3. Add 1 cup of ice and blend again until creamy.

Smooth Berries Smoothies

Ingredients:

4 cups spinach
2 celery stalks
1/2 cup of raspberries
1/2 cup of strawberries
2 bananas
1 cup ice

How you make it:

1. Place all the ingredients into blender and blend until mixture is a green juice-like consistency.

2. Add the cup of ice and blend again until creamy.

Dandelion smooth Smoothie

Ingredients:

1 small bunch dandelion greens (or substitute with spinach)
1 lemon (peeled)
2 large apples
1 banana
1 cup ice

How you make it:

1. First, Place the dandelion greens and water into blender and blend until mixture is a green juice-like consistency.
2. Stop blender and add lemon, large apple, banana and blend.
3. Add ice if desired and blend again until creamy.

Heaven Sent Smoothies

Ingredients:

6 to 8 leaves of Romaine lettuce
1/2 almond milk
2 cups water or 1 cup of ice

How you make it:

1. First, Place the lettuce and water into blender and blend until mixture is a green juice-like consistency.
2. Stop blender and add the almond milk and blend.
3. Add ice if desired and blend again until creamy.

After Cleanse Superfood Smoothies

Chocolaty city Smoothie

Here's the healthiest way to satisfy your chocolate craving any time of day! While you keep the weight after the 10 day cleanse. Enjoy this while you cleanse & Detox your Body

Ingredients:

1 cup water
11/2 cups frozen organic strawberries
1 tablespoon chia seeds
2 tablespoons raw cacao nibs
1 tablespoon raw cacao powder
6 raw macadamia nuts
3 pitted dates
1 frozen banana, cut into bite-sized chunks
1 large handful chopped kale
4 to 5 ice cubes

How you make it:

4. First, Place strawberries and water into blender and blend until mixture is a green juice-like consistency.
5. Stop blender and add cacao nibs & powder, macadamia nuts and blend for a minute.
6. Add kale with the other remaining ingredients and blend smooth.
7. Add ice if desired and blend again until creamy.

Freshly Minted Smoothie

You can use water or even coconut water if you don't want to use nut milk or almonds. The mint transforms this into another high scoring and different smoothie. Enjoy it!

Ingredients:

Handful of almonds
1 cup water
2 kiwi
¼ cup broccoli
2 dates
1 cup kale
1 cup mint
Handful of sprouts
1 tsp vanilla essence
¼ tsp salt

How you make it:

1. First, Place the almonds and water into blender and blend until mixture is a green juice-like consistency.
2. Stop blender and add dates, kiwi, kale with the other remaining ingredients and blend.
3. Add ice if desired and blend again until creamy.

Tips

Dried peaches or apricots can be used instead of dates for even more nutrition. Soak them (adding soak water too) if you want them very smooth.

Summer Ginger Smoothie

Sprouting magnifies the nutritional value of the seed and makes the nutrition more available to the biology of the body. It boosts the B-vitamin content, triples the amount of vitamin A and increases vitamin C by a factor of 5 to 6 times.

Ingredients:

1/4 cup alfalfa sprouts
1 cup baby spinach
1 cup pineapple, frozen
1/2 banana, frozen
1 cup water
1/4" – 1/2" fresh ginger, minced
1/16 teaspoon of Stevia (or agave nectar)
1-2 ice cubes, to thicken

How you make it:

1. Place all the ingredients into blender and blend until mixture is a green juice-like consistency.
2. Add the cup of ice and blend again until creamy.

Classic Dessert

This super food smoothie is indeed a classic. It is based on the famous *Vanilla Pudding* smoothie. Dance to this delicious beat, and feel your weight melt off!

Ingredients:

1 cup water
½ cup cashews (soaked if you have them available, dry will do)
3 dates (or other dried fruit)
2 tbsp. carob
1 small avocado, or half a large
1 cup mango (frozen or fresh)
2 cups mild greens
¼ - ½ tsp cinnamon
Vanilla
Pinch sea salt
Ice as desired

How you make it:

1. First, Place cashew, dates and water into blender and blend until mixture is a green juice-like consistency.
2. Stop blender and add carob, avocadoes, greens with the other remaining ingredients and blend.
3. Add ice if desired and blend again until creamy.

Tips
In this smoothie, dried peaches or apricots taste really Delicious. Soak them (adding soak water too) if you want them very smooth.

Super Green Smoothie

This smoothie houses lots of health benefits that would make you look younger, all day long. Even after the 10 day cleanse.

Ingredients:

2 stalks celery
4 cups spinach
1 apple, cored
2 bananas
1 1/2 cup of water, or enough water to blend into desired consistency.

How you make it:

1.   First, Place the spinach and water into blender and blend until mixture is a green juice-like consistency.
2.   Stop blender and add apples, bananas, greens with the other remaining ingredients and blend.
3.   Add ice if desired and blend again until creamy.

Tropical Beet Top Smoothie

Ingredients:

1 cup beet tops
2 cups spinach
1 orange, peeled and seeded
1 ripe banana
1/2 cup blueberries, fresh or frozen
1/2 small beetroot, cut into pieces
1 1/2 cups water or
1 cup of ice
Cinnamon to taste

How you make it:

1. Place all the ingredients into blender and blend until mixture is a green juice-like consistency.
2. Add the cup of ice and blend again until creamy.

Blue Dip Smoothie

If you're lucky enough to have fresh blueberries on hand you may want to throw in ½ cup of ice to the blend. Right up there with goodness, taste and score to boot.

Ingredients:

1 cup water
1 cup blueberries (frozen or fresh)
1 apple
½ cup coriander
1 stalk celery
1 1/2 cups mild greens
Sea salt
Lemon juice to taste
Ice as desired

How you make it:

1. Place all the ingredients into blender and blend until mixture is a green juice-like consistency.
2. Add ice and blend again until creamy.

Tips

To create a different experience add in a handful of mint

Crème la Crème

This smoothie is the ultimate, with a flavor sensation in its own right. And besides, you need several variations so you can keep on enjoying this one.

Ingredients:

1 cup water
½ cup cashews (soaked if you have them available, dry will do)
3 dates (or dried apricots)
1 cup mango (frozen or fresh)
1 small avocado, or half a large
2 cups mild greens
½ cup mint
2 tbsp. carob
¼ - ½ tsp cinnamon
Vanilla
Pinch sea salt
Ice as desired

How you make it:

1. First, Place cashew, dates and water into blender and blend until mixture is a green juice-like consistency.
2. Stop blender and add mango, avocados, greens with the other remaining ingredients and blend.
3. Add ice if desired and blend again until creamy.

Dandelion Devourer

Ingredients:

1/2 bunch red dandelion
1/2 small watermelon
1/2 cup strawberries
1 cup of grapes
1 cup water

How you make it:

1. Place the red dandelion and water into blender and blend until mixture is a green juice-like consistency.
2. Stop blender and add the watermelon, strawberries, grapes and blend.
3. Add ice if desired and blend again until creamy.

Loving leafy Smoothie

Some of you may want to skip the fruit in your smoothie altogether. Maybe you're trying to cut out sugars (even unrefined fruit sugar), or you're diabetic, or highly hypoglycemic. If so, try this all-green superfood smoothie that is both highly edible, nutritious and low in sugar. It also contains some necessary and nutritious fat in the form of avocado.

Ingredients:

6 leaves of red leaf lettuce
1/4 bunch of fresh basil
1/2 lime (juiced)
1/4 red onion
2 celery sticks
1/4 avocado
Stevia to taste
2 cups water

How you make it:
1.   Place all the ingredients into blender and blend until mixture is a green juice-like consistency.
2.   Add the cup of ice and blend again until creamy.

Best Anti-Aging Smoothies

Apple Allure Smoothie

This smoothie is simply smooth and classic. You know what they say; "An apple a day keeps the doctor away!" You'll have no problem meeting your daily apple quote with this delicious apple smoothie.

Ingredients:

1 frozen banana, cut into bite-sized pieces
1 organic Granny Smith apple, cored and chopped
(Keep the skin on)
1 tablespoon fresh lemon juice
1 large handful baby spinach
1 cup cold water
2 to 3 pitted dates
1/2 teaspoon cinnamon
1/8 teaspoon nutmeg
4 to 5 ice cubes

How you make it:

1. Place all the ingredients except the ice in a blender, and blend until smooth and creamy.
2. Add the ice and process again. Drink chilled.

Golden Maiden Smoothie

Delight in this not so green looking smoothie that packs a Golden punch! It contains banana, which aids anti-aging. This smoothie is so good, you would love every mouthful.

Ingredients:

½ cup raspberries
½ cup strawberries
2 bananas
1.5 cup sweet potato leaves (or other mild greens)
¼ -½ cup parsley
1 cup water
Ice as desired

How you make it:

1. Place all the ingredients into blender and blend until mixture is a green juice-like consistency.
2. Add ice and blend again until creamy.

Heavenly Greens Smoothie

Ingredients:

1 packed cup carrot tops
2 cups spinach
1 banana
1 cup strawberries with the greens attached (yes, you can eat these too!)
1/2 cup pineapple
1/2 cup mango
1 1/2 cups water or 1 cup of ice

How you make it:
1. Place all the ingredients into blender and blend until mixture is a green juice-like consistency.
2. Add the cup of ice and blend again until smooth and creamy.

Happy-Berries Smoothie

These humble ingredients mix to give you such a pleasant drink. Dried apricots have a great nutrient profile and add a beautiful caramel-type sweetness. Delicious!

Ingredients:

8 brazil nuts in 1 cup water (or use nut milk or plain water)
4 apricots (dried) chopped
1 banana (frozen or fresh)
1 cup berries (frozen)
2 cups greens (mild/mild or mild/strong)
Ice

How you make it:

1. First, Place Brazil nut and water into blender and blend until mixture is a green juice-like consistency.
2. Stop blender and add apricots, berries, greens with the other remaining ingredients and blend.
3. Add ice if desired and blend again until creamy.

Tips

Organic unsulfured dried apricots are dark in color, so it is best advised to use it when making this delicious Smoothie.

Delicious Arugula Smoothies

Ingredients:

1 small bunch of arugula leaves
1 banana
2 pears
1/2 cup frozen raspberries
2 cups water

How you make it:

1. First, Place the arugula leaves and water into blender and blend until mixture is a green juice-like consistency.
2. Stop blender and add the other remaining ingredients and blend.
3. Add ice if desired and blend again until creamy.

Diabetes/ Blood Sugar Solution Smoothies

Lovely Pear Smoothie

In this smoothie it is recommended you use kale. The rest of your 2 cup greens component is mint. When you use any green, use as much of the stalk as you can. Just get rid of the woody ends. It's not a good policy to just use the leaves as you'll miss out on a lot of nutrition and fiber. It's all good!

Ingredients:

1 cup water
1 pear
1 orange peeled
1 cup pineapple
½ cup mint
1.5 cup kale (or other mild green)
Ice as required

How you make it:

1. First, Place pear and water into blender and blend until mixture is a green juice-like consistency.
2. Stop blender and add pineapple with the other remaining ingredients and blend.
3. Add ice and blend again until creamy.

Spinach Seduction

The mango contained in this smoothie, helps a great deal to reduce blood sugar in the body. Cheers! Drink up to a healthy life.

Ingredients:

2 cups of spinach
2 stalks celery
2 sweet yellow mangoes
1 cup water or enough water to blend into the desired consistency

How you make it:

1. First, Place the spinach and water into blender and blend until mixture is a green juice-like consistency.
2. Stop blender and add the other remaining ingredients and blend.
3. Add ice if desired and blend again until creamy.

Edible Mango Smoothies

Ingredients:

4 mangoes
4 cups edible weeds (dandelion, lambsquarters, stinging nettles, purslane, etc.)
1 cup of ice or 2 cups of water

How you make it:

1.   First, Place the edible weeds and water into blender and blend until mixture is a green juice-like consistency.
2.   Stop blender and add mango and blend.
3.   Add ice if desired and blend again until creamy.

Mint Super Greens

Ingredients:

1 bunch of a mixture of greens; spinach, parsley, kale
1 bunch of fresh mint
2 oranges
1 lemon
Stevia to taste (optional)
1 cup water or ½ cup of ice

How you make it:

1. Place all the ingredients into blender and blend until mixture is a green juice-like consistency.
2. Add the cup of ice and blend again until creamy.

Mango Spicy Smoothie

Your kids will surely like this and would give this the thumbs up!

Ingredients:

Blend first
1 cup water
8 brazil nuts (or use a cup of nut milk or plain water)
½ avocado
2 cups mild greens (such as tatsoi or chickweed)
1 cup mango (frozen or fresh)
1 tsp cinnamon
½ tsp nutmeg
Vanilla
1 cup ice

How you make it:

1.   First, Place Brazil nuts and water into blender and blend until mixture is a green juice-like consistency.
2.   Stop blender and add avocado, green with the other remaining ingredients and blend.
3.   Add 1 cup of ice and blend again until creamy.

Tips

If you need more sweetness, add more mango or 2 pieces of dried fruit. You will so like the feel under the tooth. You could sweeten with stevia or agave syrup (optional). Clove or cardamom powder can deepen the spice profile for you

Energy Packed Smoothies

Cinnamon Delight

This Smoothies makes you vibrant and active all day long. Transform this orange smoothie drink into a cinnamon-lover's delight. It really is different enough and taste really good. Everyone loves a delicious smoothie.

Ingredients:

1 orange
2 dates, remove the pits
1 stalk celery
1 cup greens
1 cup water
¼ tsp or more of cinnamon
½ cup ice

How you make it:

1. Place all the ingredients into blender and blend until mixture is a green juice-like consistency.
2. Add the cup of ice and blend again until creamy.

Peach Pie Smoothies

This smoothie is really energizing. Blend up and re-vitalize your energy.

Ingredients:

4 cups spinach leaves
2 celery stalks
6 peaches
1 cup ice

How you make it:

1. Place the spinach and water into blender and blend until mixture is a green juice-like consistency.
2. Stop blender and add celery stalks, peaches and blend.
3. Add ice if desired and blend again until creamy.

Super Green Bomber

Ingredients:

1/4 cups blueberries
1/4 cups blackberries
1 banana
1/2 cups apple juice
1/3 cups raspberry sorbet

How you make it:

1. Put all ingredients into blender.

2. Blend until smoothie consistency is reached!

Classic Blitz Smoothie

Ingredients:

2 cups of broccoli (florets and/or stems), or broccoli rabe
2 cups spinach
2 oranges, peeled and quartered
2 cups pineapple, chopped
2 bananas, frozen
2 cups frozen mixed berries
1 cup oat or quinoa
Stevia or agave to taste (optional)
2 cups water/ice

How you make it:

1. Place all the ingredients into blender and blend until mixture is a green juice-like consistency.

2. Add the cup of ice and blend again until creamy.

Spicy Plum Oat Smoothie

Ingredients:

1 cup spinach, tightly packed or 2 cups loosely packed
1 cup oat quinoa or brown rice
8 plums
1 banana
½ cup dates
½ teaspoon vanilla
1 teaspoon fresh ginger
¼ teaspoon of cayenne pepper (to taste or omit completely)
2 cups non-dairy milk

How you make it:

1. Place all the ingredients into blender and blend until mixture is a green juice-like consistency.

2. Add the cup of ice and blend again until creamy.

Conclusion

Now you have gone through this Healthy weight loss book using smoothies. You should know that this cleanse is not a diet but a lifestyle, it's not a miracle smoothie, but a smoothie that helps detox from years of impurities and processed foods. This is not a quick fix and forget, if you commit for 10 days, you would surely see great result.

This cleanse can and will help with weight loss because if you commit 10 days of not eating refined sugars, sodas, processed foods, fried foods and refined carbs then the weight will happen naturally giving you more energy and motivation to lose weight. Also remember, this cleanse will not work if you start out with doubts.

Nevertheless, With this cleanse not only will you detox and lose weight but you will gain amazing results and amazing relationships with other amazing women and men aiming for the same goal you are...a healthier and sexier YOU!!!

Thank You

If you Follow the ultimate guideline provided in the 10-day Green Smoothie Cleanse By JJ SMITH, And some of the Smoothie recipes outlined in this book. You are going to be seeing great results in your body and health in just 10 days, because it is proven to work.

If you enjoyed the recipes in this book, please take the time to share your thoughts and post a positive review with 5 star rating on Amazon, it would encourage me and make me serve you better. It'd be greatly appreciated!

If you have any question or anything at all you want to know about this cleanse, you can hit me up via mail thru andrybrown@gmail.com I am always there to help you

THANK YOU!!

Other Health Related Books You Would Like

10-Day Green Smoothie Cleanse: Lose Up to 15 Pounds in 10 Days!
By JJ Smith- The Bestselling Author in Weight Loss, Get it Here>>
http://amzn.to/1lBMBWc

SUMMARY, ANALYSIS & REVIEW OF THE 10 DAY GREEN
SMOOTHIE CLEANSE

A guide to help you follow through with the cleanse and achieve greater result. Get it HERE>> http://www.amazon.com/10-Day-Green-Smoothie-Cleanse-BestSeller-ebook/dp/B00L9242AC

Other Health Related Books You Would Like

BOOKS BY BESTSELLING AUTHORS

My 10 Day Green Smoothie Cleanse Protein Recipes: 51 Clean Meal Recipes to help you After the 10 Day Smoothie cleanse!

The 10 Days Green Smoothie Cleanse is a Phenomenal Program created to help people lose weight in 10 Days. This program is so powerful and life changing, that lots of people have achieved weight loss.

However, it is sometimes difficult to maintain the weight loss after the 10 day green smoothie cleanse, and that's why we have prepared high-protein meals to Assist with weight loss after the cleanse. In this Book you'll discover lots of High protein recipes that are healthy, clean, and delicious!

Get it HERE>> http://www.amazon.com/Green-Smoothie-Cleanse-Protein-Recipes-ebook/dp/B00KDQZH2C

The Tapping Solution for Weight Loss and Body Confidence is a powerful system that releases the emotions and beliefs that hold us back from loving our bodies. I use tapping on a regular basis and have personally benefitted from this powerful method. It's one of the most important practices in my healing arsenal.

Get The The Ultimate Tapping Solution Guide: Using EFT to tap your way to WEIGHT LOSS, Wealth and Build Body Confidence for Women

Click Here>> Amazon U.S Link>> http://www.amazon.com/Ultimate-Tapping-Solution-Guide-Confidence-ebook/dp/B00K6JB97S

Books on Health & Fitness Diets

RECOMMENDED BOOK FOR WEIGHT LOSS AND DIET:

My 10-Day Smoothie Cleanse & Detox Diet Cookbook: Burn the Fat, Lose weight Fast and Boost your Metabolism for Busy Mom, Restart your life with this cookbook and experience an amazing transformation of your body and your health. I am really excited for you!

CLICK HERE TO BUY: http://www.amazon.com/10-Day-Detox-Diet-Cookbook-Metabolism-ebook/dp/B00IRE3CV0

Get this bestselling Grain Brain Book- **My brain against all grain Cookbook: 61 Easy-to-make Healthy Foods that would help you stick to the Grain-Brain-free Diet!** Discover The Surprising Truth about Wheat, Carbs, and Sugar--Your Brain's Silent Killers

Amazon US Link: http://www.amazon.com/dp/B00J9DX3X0

Amazon UK Link: http://www.amazon.co.uk/dp/B00J9DX3X0

The Coconut Diet Cookbook: Using Coconut Oil to Lose weight FAST, Supercharge Your Metabolism & Look Beautiful!

Link **http://www.amazon.com/dp/B00K1IIOGS**

39225923R00076

Made in the USA
Lexington, KY
11 February 2015